Mindfulness

Beginners Guide on How to Shut Off
Your Brain and Stay in the Moment

Free membership into the Mastermind Self Development Group!

For a limited time, you can join the Mastermind Self Development Group for free! You will receive videos and articles from top authorities in self development as well as a special group only offers on new books and training programs. There will also be a monthly member only draw that gives you a chance to win any book from your Kindle wish list!

If you sign up through this link http://www.mastermindselfdevelopment.com/specialreport you will also get a special free report on the Wheel of Life. This report will give you a visual look at your current life and then take you through a series of exercises that will help you plan what your perfect life looks like. The workbook does not end there; we then take you through a process to help you plan how to achieve that perfect life. The process is very powerful and has the potential to change your life forever. Join the group now and start to change your life!
http://www.mastermindselfdevelopment.com/specialreport

Table of Contents

Introduction

Chapter 1: The Value of Mindfulness

Chapter 2: Creating the Calm

Chapter 3: Peace in Pandemonium

Chapter 4: The Practical Practice

Chapter 5: Maintaining Mindfulness

Conclusion

Introduction

Thank you and congratulations on purchasing this book! "*Mindfulness:* Beginners Guide on How to Shut Off Your Brain and Stay in the Moment" is a book written specifically for individuals who want to become more mindful, but who have a hard time encouraging their brain to be quiet. While you may feel as though mindfulness is not the technique for you, the truth is that everyone who has mastered mindfulness at one point or another had the exact same difficulty!

This book has been carefully crafted to bring resolutions for all who are struggling to achieve mindfulness in their lives. The wording and instructions are created in an easy-to-understand method that will allow you to understand the simplicity of being mindful, and how you can effortlessly draw it into your own life.

Mindfulness is a highly valuable tool that has the ability to achieve many things in a person's life. Whether you are seeking to add value to each day, eliminate the stress of worrying, or improve your quality of life, you can achieve all of that through mindfulness. In this book, you will be guided on how to achieve mindfulness on an average day, even if you are experiencing a particularly large amount of chaos or stress that may be causing you to feel extra edgy.

It is important to remember that mindfulness is a practice. Once you learn how to be mindful, you will have an easy time re-learning it. You will need to make sure you take the time each day to practice mindfulness, even when you become a master at it. Mindfulness is a balancing act where we are continually practicing our ability to stay in tune. Sometimes, you may notice that you have not been practicing mindfulness in your life. The result may show up as added stress, less mental involvement in day to day life, less clarity on what you are doing from moment to moment, and less quality of time spent with those around you. If you notice this is happening, the best thing you can do is become mindful of the existence of the chaos, and allow yourself to realign with a mindful state and start practicing your techniques again. In this book, you are going to learn exactly how you can do that.

Being mindful may feel difficult, especially for beginners. It is not natural in this day and age to tune out from the rest of the world and narrow in on what is happening in the moment. However, once you understand and implement this valuable technique in your life, you will notice that you feel your stress levels reduce significantly. You will also experience life greater, and with more joy. If you are ready to dive into learning about mindfulness, you are ready to begin chapter one.

Chapter 1: The Value of Mindfulness

Throughout history, a huge number of people have practiced mindfulness. As such, we see it across many religions and many other areas of culture. Mindfulness is a simple practice that, when practiced regularly, allows for humans to stay more focused on the specific task at hand, and resist the temptation to worry about or become absorbed in events of the past or the unpredictable future.

Mindfulness is a relatively simple task to learn once you understand exactly what it is and how you can use it in your daily life. This precious technique has the ability to add value to your life in many ways. Those who practice mindfulness on a regular basis notice increased happiness, greater synchronicity with themselves and the world around them, and even health improvements. Mindfulness truly is a valuable technique that has the ability to offer you a number of different benefits.

Emotional Benefits

Many people report a high number of emotional benefits that come from practicing mindfulness in their daily lives, and it makes sense as to why. Being mindful and staying present in the moment allows for people to experience the greatest benefit of each experience in life. Because of this heightened involvement in the experience, people report a greater result from it. The more involved they are in the moment, mentally, the more they understand about the moment and the more value they gain from it. This is because they are not renting any of their mind space out to unnecessary or irrelevant thoughts or emotions for the present moment. They are taking the time to notice every element of the experience, draw in all that it has to offer, and really take a heightened value from it. Because of this, people report feeling more peaceful, less stressed, happier, and a more genuine sense of joy that comes from being mindful.

Look at the below example to gain a greater understanding as to how mindfulness can change a situation:

Situation 1: *Sally was spending time with her Dad, as they often did on Fridays after school. He liked to pick her up and take her out for her favorite treat: ice cream. Sally loved spending the extra time with her Dad, but he always seemed distant. He would regularly check his watch or his phone, and often didn't listen to what hear her at all. Even though she loved having that one-on-one time, she wished her Dad would stop worrying about his work and pay more attention to her.*

Above, you can see that Sally's Dad was not being mindful. His frequent checking of his watch and his phone signified that he was somewhere else in his mind. Sometimes, he was so distant, he didn't even hear her talking! This can be damaging to relationships with other people and can lead to stress, discomfort, anger, and other unnecessary issues between two people. This is not a good state to be in, especially considering Sally is talking about her own Dad!

Situation 2: *Sally was spending time with her Dad, as they often did on Fridays after school. He liked to pick her up and take her out for her favorite treat: ice cream. Sally loved spending extra time with her Dad. He always gave her all of the attention she needed and wanted during this time. He would talk to her about how her day went, ask her how school was doing, and even offer to help her practice more for the cheerleading team! Sally knew he was a busy man because of his demanding job, so she really appreciated that he took the time to put his work aside and give her his full attention for their time together.*

Above, Sally's Dad was being mindful. He was actively involved in the moment, he was listening to his daughter and engaging in meaningful conversation with her. He put away his phone and stopped checking his watch, and he really gave his daughter the quality time that they both needed. This time would nurture their relationship together, and create a more powerful and meaningful bond between the father and daughter, which is valuable for both of them.

Being mindful has the ability to offer a significant number of emotional benefits. The more mindful you are, the more present you are in the moment. This makes your experiences much more valuable and can help bring you more joy, a greater sense of connection, reduced stress, and greater fulfillment in life.

Health Benefits

Believe it or not, mindfulness does have actual physical health benefits. The more mindful you are in life, the healthier you are going to be. While this phenomenal technique isn't so powerful that it can cure ailments, it does have the ability to prevent and reduce the occurrence of a number of symptoms and diseases. There's a very practical and logical reason as to why, too.

When you are mindful, you are present in the moment. This translates to a number of different benefits that contribute to the increased quality of health that can be drawn from being a mindful person. First, being more present in the moment means that you are less stressed and agitated. Remember all of the emotional benefits you learned about a moment ago? Someone who is in a less stressed and calmer state of mind is much less likely to experience common symptoms and diseases that are born from stress. These include but are not limited to: high blood pressure; headaches; tense muscles; a sore jaw; and even some cardiac ailments. Stress has the ability to cause a number of different diseases in our body. While becoming less stressed isn't the *only* way to prevent or eliminate these ailments and diseases, it is a great way to reduce your risk of getting them to begin with. It can also assist you in eliminating them when used alongside a qualified health plan set out by your health provider.

In addition to allowing you to eliminate or at least reduce symptoms and diseases, mindfulness can also allow you to be more in sync with your body. When this occurs, you will be much more likely to take care of your body in the way it needs to be taken care of. For example, if you are thirsty, you will drink water. If you are hungry, you will eat. If you are mindful, you are likely going to choose a healthy and fulfilling food option over a sugary-filled quick-fix to your hunger. If you are sleepy, you will go to bed. So on, and so forth. The more mindful you are, the more in sync with your body you will be, and the more likely you will take care of it in a way that keeps it healthy and working optimally. Additionally, if you notice something wrong, you will be able to schedule an appointment with your doctor right away, as opposed to ignoring it for several weeks because you are unaware of it at first.

As you can see, mindfulness has a high number of health benefits, beyond emotional ones. When you are mindful, you reduce your risk of contracting ailments and diseases that can greatly decrease your quality of life, or in extreme cases, kill you. This practice is a wonderful technique to stay in tune with your body, listen to what it needs, and nourish it in ways that allow you to flourish and work in the most optimal way.

Worldly Benefits

If you thought mindfulness only had a benefit on yourself, you were wrong! Mindfulness is a practical and strategic way to benefit the world around you, as well! This amazing technique allows you the opportunity to improve your world through several different ways.

First, when you are mindful, you are much less likely to engage in arguments or conflict with other people. When you do choose to engage in a conflict, you will be much more rational about your approach, and the situation will likely diffuse quickly. If it doesn't, you will recognize that no benefit is being drawn from the experience, and you will remove yourself from the situation. Mindful people are generally much less emotionally charged in a negative format than those who are not mindful. They are more likely to be able to handle anger and stresses strategically, which means that even their "opponent" will end the situation in a more calm and rational way. This may simply diffuse one set of bad emotions, or it could trickle and encourage the other person to go learn about mindfulness and practice being more peaceful and calm in their own lives. You never know!

Additionally, the more we are in sync with the world around us, the more we are going to experience value from the world, and give value to the world. We are more likely to notice people who are struggling, so we can offer help. We are more likely to experience the highest joy we possibly can, which truly is contagious! Many other people who experience your intoxicating joy are going to turn around and experience some of their own as a result!

Finally, people who are mindful are generally a lot more considerate of the Earth itself. They tend to take better care of the world around them through many measures, including but not limited to: recycling, not littering, helping clean up after others, taking care of plants and animals, and more! Doing all of this contributes to the healthy production and growth of the planet, which means that you are assisting it in thriving and maintaining its health!

Being a mindful person adds greater value to life, for the person who is mindful both emotionally and mentally, for the people around them, and for the Earth itself. When people are mindful, they are less stressed and more at peace, they are more engaged with those around them, and they are much more likely to experience greater fulfillment out of their lives. This practice and technique is potentially one of the most valuable ones you could ever teach yourself.

Chapter 2: Creating the Calm

The very first step in becoming more mindful in your life is learning to create the calmness. Or, in other words, learning to relax your mind and let things be. In this chapter, you will learn exactly how you can let go of everything that is stressing you out from your past and your future, and focus strictly on the present moment. This is really the biggest lesson in mindfulness that you need to learn. Once you learn what mindfulness is and how it feels, you will have a much easier time applying it to various situations throughout your life.

Learning to be mindful is truly a process. You are going to start out and probably have a hard time with it at first, and then you are going to continue practicing it until you are a master at it. Once you learn how to become mindful the first time, practicing mindfulness constantly becomes easier every single time you practice it. So, if you ever find you've gone a few days particularly stressed out and lacking mindfulness, you will know exactly what you need to do in order to reclaim your peace through mindfulness.

The first thing is understanding exactly what mindfulness is. Essentially, mindfulness is a form of being present in the moment. It is a time where you prevent yourself from becoming absorbed in thoughts of the past or the perceived future, and you let yourself experience exactly what is materializing right in front of you, right in that moment. So, you are noticing the colors of your surroundings, the smells, the feelings, the tastes if there are any, and the sounds. You really want to enrich as many of your senses with each experience as you possibly can, *and* take the time to actually notice them.

The easiest way to become mindful in a moment is to practice the 5-4-3-2-1 technique. This technique became popular within the last few years for good reason. It is an excellent way to help reclaim your current moment and encourage your mind to focus on what is physically going on around you, rather than straying away into other parts of your mind. In order to practice this method, all you have to do is quietly tell yourself five things you can see, four things you can touch, three things you can hear, two things you can smell and one thing you can taste. This helps you focus on exactly what is happening in the present, and keeps your mind actively paying attention to your current experiences.

You should practice this technique any time you want to become mindful of the moment around you. Observing your experiences with all of your senses is a great way to fully immerse yourself in the present and truly gain all of the value it has to offer. The more you practice this, the easier it will become for you.

You may be wondering when you should use mindfulness. Of course, it's not practical to expect that you are going to be mindful every minute of every day. Even mindfulness masters can't do that, so no matter how long and hard you practice, you are going to experience moments where your mind strays away from you. That is completely normal and absolutely okay. The human brain is a natural wanderer and part of being mindful and experiencing life as fully as possible is recognizing that and giving your brain the permission to do so. The goal is not to have you constantly having to stop your brain from doing what it naturally wants to do. Instead, it's controlling your brain to not wander when the situation warrants for you to be present. When you are working, when you are waking up, when you are eating something new, when you are spending time with people you love, and many other situations are more fully experienced when you practice mindfulness while doing so. However, that's not to say that you can never allow your mind to wander. In this short list below, you will learn more techniques about mindfulness and when you should apply this strategy in your life.

Give Yourself Mind Permission to Wander

Since your mind naturally wants to wander, sometimes the best way to become mindful is to let your mind wander. This may sound counterproductive, but the reality is that it will actually save and enhance your mindfulness practice. When your mind wants to wander and you're consistently having to tell it no, you are not going to be practicing mindfulness because you will instead be having an internal conflict with your mind. Rather than allowing that to go on and then stressing yourself out further, you can simply give yourself permission to let your mind wander. You can let it go for a set period of time, say like five minutes, and then when that time is up, you can gently bring your mind back to the present moment and carry on with your mindfulness practice. This sounds like a paradox, but sometimes being mindful of your desire to let your mind wander is the best way to do it!

Practice Mindfulness During Regular Routines

Often times, our regular routines become mundane and repetitive. We do them so often that we no longer think about what we're doing, we just do it. You may notice this to be the case for many instances in your day and life, for example: brushing your teeth, driving to work, large portions of your work day, coming home from work, making supper, and more. These are all a great time to practice being mindful. When we tend to "check out" for these activities, we can stop feeling present in the moment and start working on autopilot. Not only does this detract from mindfulness, but it can actually lead to your emotional run-down, and sometimes even dangerous situations, such as if you are on mental autopilot while driving to work. These are some of the best times to practice being mindful. You may find that your routine is a lot more fun than you were experiencing, or that there are new and more efficient ways you could be doing things!

Switch It Up!

If you are feeling that your life is too full of routines, another great way to practice mindfulness and really gain a lot of value from it is to switch up your routines! If you always wake up, stretch, go to the bathroom, turn on the coffee pot and then flick on the morning news, then try something else for a change! Wake up, go to the bathroom, set the kettle to boil and make yourself a nice beverage and then drink it on the balcony! You may choose to take a different route to work, walk a different way to your office, sit down in a different way, or do any number of different things to help switch up the pace of things. When you break the routine, you give your mind a bit of a break from the autopilot mode and you encourage it to pay attention by making it interested in what is going on. Sometimes becoming mindful of your routine and during your routines will actually lead you to make changes because you will realize you have been doing unnecessary extras, or that certain things aren't as efficient or effective anymore. Being mindful and giving yourself permission to switch it up is a great way to get your brain active in your daily routines again and give it a break from the regular day-to-day activities that can become boring and mundane.

Practice Mindfulness as Soon as You Wake

When we wake up, many of us don't jump straight out of bed. Even if you do, it is still a great time to practice mindfulness. Since you have been asleep for a while, you have been on somewhat of a mental vacation from your body. During this time, your brain has been wandering for several hours, typically. So, this is a great time to practice mindfulness! See if you can notice the light shining in through the window, the sensation of the blankets or the air on your skin, the sound of the birds or of other people in your home, and any smells and tastes you may notice.

The morning is a great time to practice mindfulness because it allows you to start your day off with being more aware of your surroundings. They say that when we start our day out a certain way, it can make it easier to carry on that task throughout the rest of the day. With that logic, if you are mindfulness first thing in the morning, you will likely find it much easier to be mindful throughout the rest of your day. It is a great way to set the tone, have a positive morning, and really create the perfect setting to allow the rest of your day to be mindful and peaceful.

Short and Sweet Wins the Treat

Remember how you learned that mindfulness isn't something that you are expected to, or even capable of, practicing for every minute of the day? If you struggle with mindfulness, sometimes it's easiest just to be mindful in short bursts. In fact, science has proven that if you are mindful for short periods several times during the day as opposed to one single longer period, you will gain greater benefit from it. With that knowledge, it is a good idea to allow yourself to become present for a few minutes at a time throughout your entire day, instead of expecting yourself to become mindful about everything you do all of the time, or only practicing it once a day for lengthy time frames. Being mindful doesn't have to be a long and hard technique that you put a significant amount of effort into for several hours each day. Instead, draw your mind in when you remember to, and practice doing it more and more each day.

Practice Mindfulness When You're Waiting

When we are waiting for things, we tend to become stressed out, bored, or even agitated. Most humans do not like to wait, which means that this is a great time for you to practice mindfulness! Instead of letting your mind wander down the rabbit hole of negativity that leads you to feel uncomfortable and upset about a situation that you can't control, practice being calm and peaceful. Notice the other people in the lineup, recognize that you're all waiting together, listen to the sounds around you, see what else you can notice about the particular situation. You will be surprised at how enjoyable it can be to stop and observe those around us during these periods where we're forced to wait. You can even do this if you're waiting to be taken off of hold on the phone, when you're waiting for an appointment in a lobby, or at any other time that you find yourself waiting around. It is a great chance to regroup and reframe an otherwise bland, or even stressful activity!

Assign a Reminder Prompt to Help You

Many people find it extremely helpful to associate something with mindfulness and use it as an opportunity to remind themselves to be mindful. There are many ways you may do this in your life, and how you personally choose to do it will be unique to you. However, it can be extremely beneficial to have something that you associate with mindfulness that will prompt you to practice mindfulness throughout your day. Some people choose something simple such as a bracelet or a certain trinket they carry around in their pocket, so that any time they touch, see or notice the item, they are reminded to practice mindfulness. In this day and age, we are also granted with the gift of technology. If you find having a trinket around with you doesn't remind you to stay mindful, you may prefer to set reminders in your phone or switch your phone background to something that will prompt you to practice mindfulness throughout the day. However, you choose to do it, having these prompts are a great way to remember to practice mindfulness and infuse it into your everyday life. Again, you don't have to practice mindfulness constantly, but practicing it in short bursts several times throughout the day is an excellent way to increase the value you gain from mindfulness, emotionally, physically, and otherwise.

Practice Meditation

Meditation is essentially a prolonged practice of mindfulness. Many people love using meditation as a means to infuse an even higher quality of mindfulness into their daily routines. Meditation is an excellent opportunity to objectively explore the thoughts in your mind and guide yourself to a new state of calm. This is especially helpful if you feel that something has been bugging you for a while. Meditation may seem difficult, especially to a beginner, but it is actually quite simple. In order to practice meditation, all you need to do is give yourself a set amount of time, set a timer on your phone if you need to, and then close your eyes and release your control over your mind. Every time you notice your mind has wandered "too far", you can gently practice bringing it back to the center. Some choose to hold an image in their mind, and when their thoughts wander, at any time that they've noticed it's happened, they gently bring their mind back to the thought of the image. You may find that your mind wanders a lot, or that it can be hard to even realize that it has done so. This is completely natural, and you will experience this for the majority of your meditation practices, even when you become a master at it. The best thing you can do is give yourself the permission to practice meditation without judging yourself for how you do so.

The Conclusion

Mindfulness is an ongoing practice that you will learn about as you continue to practice the techniques you have been provided with here. You may realize that it is hard at first, but in time you will get much better at it. Remember, there are going to be times that you struggle with mindfulness, even when you are a master. The best way to keep yourself on the path of mindfulness is to set reminders and encourage yourself to practice mindfulness, especially during mundane and routine activities that we generally set ourselves to "autopilot" for us to complete. You will likely find that the more you practice, the easier it is to remember to do so. Like other skills, mindfulness is one you will master if you practice it often enough. This way, if you ever find that you have gone a prolonged period of time without mindfulness, it will be easy to draw it back into your life and pick up where you left off. This practice is not meant to be a stressful one or one that you worry about having to learn. Instead, it is one that will help you learn more about yourself and the world around you, while in turn providing you with significant benefits related to your health, your emotions, your mental wellbeing, and even the world around you.

Chapter 3: Peace in Pandemonium

There is one specific time when you may want to practice mindfulness, but you are having a difficult time. This is one of the hardest points to master mindfulness, and once you do so, you'll know that you are mindfulness master. The hardest time to practice and maintain mindfulness is when you are experiencing any form of conflict. Whether your conflict is internal with yourself, external with another human, or external with the environment you're in, conflict can create a great difficulty when it comes to practicing mindfulness. Consequently, it is one of the best times to practice mindfulness, as well.

The moment you notice you are in a situation that involves conflict, regardless of what type of conflict, you are going to want to use your learned practice to infuse mindfulness into the situation. This is going to quickly allow you to rationalize your emotions, adjust your action, and likely diffuse the situation quickly. You will enable yourself and that which you are in conflict with the gift of being respected and appreciated as it is, free of judgment. You allow yourself the permission to recognize the situation, honor your discomfort, and respond in such a way that allows all parties to be at peace with the resolution. Mindfulness during conflict is one of the most powerful ways to turn a difficult situation into something easier to manage. You are about to learn exactly how you can practice mindfulness during a difficult or conflicting situation, and how it is going to benefit your life in many ways beyond what simple daily mindfulness can do on its own.

The following acronym "RAIN" is a great skill to practice when you are experiencing conflict. This simple acronym will allow you to regain your mindfulness practice and use it as a means to eliminate the conflict you are currently experiencing. When you practice this, you will likely find that at first that it can be difficult. After you become used to using it, however, you will probably find that it becomes easier, or even second nature whenever you are being faced with conflict. The simplicity of this acronym makes it easy to remember, even during a hard situation, and can help you quickly diffuse the situation at hand.

Recognize the Conflict

The first and most important part of practicing mindfulness during conflict is recognizing that the conflict is occurring. You are likely not going to have the time or desire to practice the 5-4-3-2-1 strategy, as conflict is usually fast and heated. Instead, simply take the time to recognize the conflict. You should then give yourself a moment to become aware of your personal sensations. What are you feeling in your body and in your mind? What emotions are you bringing into this experience that may be making it harder for you to be rational? You may want to form judgments around these thoughts or feelings or try and ignore them because they are unpleasant, but the reality is that you need to recognize them, and the best way to do so is to eliminate judgment and simply just recognize as much as you can.

Once you recognize your thoughts and emotions, as well as physical experiences, it will be easier to give them a label. Often when we are in conflict, the only emotion we feel we are experiencing is anger. Generally, that is not the case. We are instead feeling a number of emotions, or one particularly strong emotion that is uncomfortable and often mislabeled as anger. It could be jealousy, hurt, sadness, worry, or any other number of emotions. Recognizing the exact emotions that you experience will give you the opportunity to address them appropriately. It also gives you an opportunity to have a greater awareness of yourself, and potentially learn some important things about yourself that you may not have learned about otherwise.

Allow Yourself (and Others) To Own Their Opinion

Once you have recognized the situation, your personal sensations and emotions, and the particular underlying emotion or emotions that you are experiencing, you need to practice "allowing". This means that you are just allowing life to be. You allow yourself to have your right to your opinion, and you allow others to do the same. You should allow yourself to have the experience of the negative emotions, even if it hurts, and allow yourself to learn from what the emotions are trying to teach you. A great way to give yourself permission to allow things to happen as they are is to mentally say "yes" to your emotions. Allow yourself to accept your emotions as they are, and allow them to be experienced fully. Doing this is going to give you the opportunity to quickly and completely address the emotions in the situation, rather than bottling them up and drawing them out later at an equally destructive time.

Investigate the Situation

Sometimes when you recognize the situation and allow the emotions to be felt and allow yourself to simply experience life, you will feel the conflict quickly fade. Other times, it may persist. If you are experiencing a type of conflict that is particularly persistent and you are having a hard time managing it, you may want to move on to the step called "investigate". This gives you the ability to further explore the situation and grow from it. The following questions are a great way to help yourself address emotions, especially if you are not sure exactly what you are feeling, as well as address the situation, especially if you are not sure of exactly what has happened:

1. "What is the tone of the experience?" (Negative, neutral, or positive)
2. "What specific event triggered this conflict?"
3. "What about this event made it triggering to me?"
4. "Have there been similar events in the past that triggered me before?"
5. "What is the story that I am telling myself about these particular feelings?"
6. "What is the story that these particular feelings are trying to tell me?"
7. "Are there any alternative stories that exist for these feelings I am experiencing?"
8. "Is the story I am telling myself actually realistic?"
9. "Do I have any bodily sensations connected to this particular experience?"

The more you investigate, the more you are going to learn from the situation. You will often find surprising and interesting answers that help draw you deeper into your own existence and understand why certain things make you feel certain ways, especially if they seem to be a trend. This will allow you to become more mindful of the conflict itself, but will also allow you to become more mindful of you as a person and how you can nurture yourself in a way that will reduce or eliminate these conflicts going forward.

If you are having a hard time discovering the emotional attachments to the conflict, or are unsure as to why they are affecting you, it can be a good idea to address these with a series of investigation questions. This will allow you to gain greater clarity on the situation and respond in a better way in the future.

Non-Identification from the Situation

While this step is not a step that you take action on, it is one that is involved in the conflict-resolution process when using mindfulness. You will know you have successfully used mindfulness in your conflicting situation when you are no longer identifying with the situation. Instead of saying things like "why me?" or "what did I do to deserve this?", you will be in a position where you understand the conflict and recognize it was simply a difficult situation. Your perspective will be shifted, and you will notice that you no longer identify with the situation and that you instead recognize it for what it is, allow it to be, and carry on.

Mindfulness can be particularly hard when you are in a conflicting situation. It can be easy to become immersed in the feelings you are experiencing and feed into them, whether they are ones of sadness, anger, hurt, or other difficult emotions. When we feel these, we tend to ignore *why* and focus more on eliminating them through action. That is why we often associate yelling, screaming, temper tantrums, and other negative elimination actions with these emotions. The more we get stuck in our heads and fail to address the situation in a mindful manner, the deeper it seeds into our bodies and makes it harder for us to respond in any other way. That is why it is crucial that you practice mindfulness, especially during conflicting situations.

Added Health Benefits of Mindfulness During Conflict

As mentioned previously, there are added benefits of practicing mindfulness during conflicting situations. These benefits are largely related to mental health and have a lasting value in our lives. The first way mindfulness during conflict benefits you is that it essentially trains your brain to react in a more peaceful and rational way with certain triggers. This allows your brain to learn new patterns that will make it easier for you to act with mindfulness in future conflicting situations. The more you practice mindfulness during conflict, the easier it will become!

The second way that mindfulness helps during conflict is by allowing you to address your internal experiences related to specific triggers. This gives you the ability to look deeper within' yourself and truly understand why things are difficult for you. The more you practice understanding your conflicts on this deeper level, the more you are going to understand yourself and the greater your mindfulness practice will be. It will also give you the ability to work through residual triggers and make it easier for you to eliminate those triggers altogether, so you won't have to worry about them coming up for you anymore!

You are halfway done!

Congratulations on making it to the halfway point of the journey. Many try and give up long before even getting to this point, so you are to be congratulated on this. You have shown that you are serious about getting better every day. I am also serious about improving my life, and helping others get better along the way. To do this I need your feedback. Click on the link below and take a moment to let me know how this book has helped you. If you feel there is something missing or something you would like to see differently, I would love to know about it. I want to ensure that as you and I improve, this book continues to improve as well. Thank you for taking the time to ensure that we are all getting the most from each other.

Chapter 4: The Practical Practice

Despite what you have already learned, there are many more ways still to practice mindfulness in your life. The more practical the application is, the easier it will be to practice and the more you are going to learn from it. For some people, setting aside time to practice mindfulness every day is simply not something they are willing to do. While it can be beneficial to do so, there are other even more practical ways to infuse mindfulness into your day, should you decide you prefer to do it that way.

In this chapter, we are going to further explore the practicality of mindfulness, and how you can use it in your day to day life. These simple moments in your life are a great time to practice mindfulness and really draw the best value from it that you possibly can. When you are practicing mindfulness, you may wish to start with a very practical application, then gradually increase the amount of time you spend practicing this habit. Whichever way you choose to do it, it is completely up to you!

Be Mindful When You Eat

Many of us are in such a rush that when we eat, we plow through our meals as quickly as we can. The experience of food has been largely lost on us, especially in modern times where fast-paced life and fast-paced food are the norm. One of the best times you can introduce mindfulness into your day is while you are eating. Being mindful when you eat is an incredible way to turn eating into a pleasurable experience. You will learn what exactly you like and what you don't like, you will give yourself the chance to thoroughly taste the foods you are eating, and you will allow yourself the opportunity to truly enjoy the experience of eating. As well, when you are full, you will recognize that and stop eating, which means you will always feel satisfied and fulfilled after a meal, instead of overfull or uncomfortable. Many people who choose to eat mindfully find that they stay away from foods that are distasteful and unhealthy, like fast foods, and start to enjoy more quality foods, as well.

You don't have to reserve mindfulness for the process of eating, alone, either. You can also practice mindfulness when you are cooking. Take time to observe all of the colors and scents coming together, notice the way the food looks as it becomes closer and closer to being completed. The more you invest in being mindful during your eating experience, the more enjoyable eating is going to be. A great reason to practice mindfulness during your meals is that in doing so, you will spend more time paying attention to your body. That way, when you are full, you will finish. You may notice you become full much sooner than you'd previously thought. This is a great way to stay healthy and allow your body the opportunity to take a break once it's done. Many people who eat mindfully find that they no longer gorge themselves on meals and that they enjoy themselves a lot more. Cooking and eating are a great opportunity to practice mindfulness and truly experience the joy and satisfaction that food has to offer when it is appreciated appropriately.

When You're Dwelling On the Past

Virtually everyone spends time thinking about the past, and at one time or another, we've all caught ourselves dwelling on it. The past is something that can be a valuable learning tool, but it can also detract from our present and future if we start to dwell on it. Many people stop using the past as a learning experience and start using it as a punishment to keep themselves from repeating things they did in the past that caused pain in their lives. What this does is harm them every single time they decide to invest more of their valuable time and emotion into this thought. The best thing you can do when this is happening is become mindful.

Being mindful about your past, particularly when you are dwelling on it, means that you will spend time recognizing that it is in the past. Instead of using it as a weapon against yourself or a punishment, you will start to use it as an opportunity to learn and grow. You will recognize why it hurt you, and what has made you cling on to that experience for so long. You will also have the opportunity to learn how you get through difficult times, and how they can assist you with growth. It won't necessarily make it easier to overcome future internal conflicts, but it will definitely give you a blueprint to effectively get there.

While Driving

Many people these days spend a great deal of time in our cars. Unfortunately, a lot of people also become so used to driving that they are no longer mindful of the experience itself. This is why many accidents happen: people become what we like to call "over confident" and they get into an accident. In other words, they became so used to driving that they stopped paying as much attention and respecting the danger that coincides with driving. A great way to change this up is to practice mindfulness while you are driving. When you are driving, you can practice mindfulness by spending more time noticing what is around you, paying attention to your mirrors, and watching your speed. You can take a few deep breaths when you're at stoplights and regroup yourself. Sometimes, a great way to enhance your mindfulness when driving is to turn off the music and really pay attention to the moment around you. This change in the familiar sound that fills your car can really help trigger you to become more mindful. Using time spent driving in your car is a great opportunity to practice mindfulness, as well as eliminate the "overconfidence" factor that can be a major risk when people are too comfortable with their driving patterns and routines.

When You Arrive at Work

So many people arrive at work and immediately become stressed out. In fact, they become stressed out on their way to work. This stress is often not provoked by anything aside from simply arriving at work. For many people, the workplace is an emotional trigger to experience stress or some other uncomfortable emotion. A great opportunity for practicing mindfulness is when you first arrive at work. Take time to notice how you are feeling, and what sort of physical sensations are attached to those feelings. Then, you can also take the time to consider why those feelings occur, and how they are truly affecting your day-to-day life. The reality is, many of us, if not all of us, have to work and keep our jobs. Since that is a factor we cannot change, it is not valuable to allow it to cause us significant stress and internal turmoil each day. Instead, you can address these emotions and practice mindfulness to allow yourself to realistically perceive the experience and draw more enjoyment out of your working experiences.

On Your Work Break

Another great time to ground yourself is when you're taking a break at work. This mindfulness experience allows you to regroup from any stress that your work may have caused up until that point, and then start working again with a new, more peaceful frame of mind. Being mindful at work is very important because this is where many of us tend to draw stress from. The more you are able to become mindful of your experiences, shift your focus and perspective, and learn to enjoy your working experience, the less stressful the workplace is going to become for you. A great way to do this is on your breaks.

Alternatively, if you are having a particularly stressful day, it can be beneficial to take a short unscheduled break to practice mindfulness. You can do this in a simple two-minute trip to the washroom. All you need to do is head into the bathroom, and start practicing your mindfulness. You can use the 5-4-3-2-1 method to ground yourself and keep yourself in the present moment. In the process, it will let you take a second to regroup and shift your focus to something more positive that is associated with your work. This is a great way to relieve sudden and urgent stressors that can arise while we are at work.

It is a really good idea to spend a few minutes out of your work day focusing on mindfulness. This is the perfect opportunity to quickly relieve ourselves from stressful emotions and thoughts and allow ourselves to become present in the moment and remember the bigger picture. Doing this will make your workplace less stressful, and help make arriving at work a more enjoyable experience for you.

Grounding Yourself with Noise

We all hear a lot of noise during the day: phones ringing, doorbells chiming, the sounds of cars going by, and so many other sounds. These are all a great opportunity to practice mindfulness. When you are busy with something, you may notice that these sounds all sort of drop to the background and are no longer something you recognize. You should take the opportunity to recognize these sounds whenever you can, and allow yourself to use them as a prompt to quickly ground yourself. Bring yourself back into the present moment, recognize what is going on around you, and become mindful of your current situation. Most often, this is a great way to alleviate stress and become more present each day. You can use this when you are working, when you are at home, or at any other time during your day when you are preoccupied with your thoughts and want to become more focused on the present moment and the world around you.

Leaving Work

Due to many people working jobs, the workplace truly becomes a great opportunity for practicing mindfulness. Perhaps one of the things that makes this the best place is because it is also the place that most people associate with high-stress levels. This may be because the workplace is a place where we all feel pressure to attend in order to maintain our lifestyles, but many of us are not passionate about our jobs. It can lead to a very mundane, boring, and unhappy experience for many people who are going to work. Even if you don't totally dislike your job or have any particular experiences there that cause you to be able to pinpoint your stress to any one thing, it can still become an unhappy place if you are not inspired by it and passionate about the work you are doing.

Practicing mindfulness is a great way to change that. Since you are already practicing when you arrive and when you are on breaks, it makes sense that another great time to practice mindfulness is when you leave work. Doing this gives you the amazing opportunity of leaving behind the days' stressors and appreciating the current moment. At the moment you leave, you no longer have to worry about work duties until you come back. With that knowledge, you should spend time each day practicing mindfulness and leaving your work stressors behind so you can arrive home with a fresh state of mind. Doing this will make your home time much less stressful and more rejuvenating, making it easier to arrive at work the next time you are scheduled to do so.

Arriving Home from A Day Out

Another excellent time to practice mindfulness is when you arrive back home after being away for some time. You may be away due to work, shopping, a trip away, or any other number of things. Regardless of the reason, this is a great opportunity to practice mindfulness. Take a moment to notice the comfort of your home, the familiar surroundings around you, the people or animals that are there to greet you, and anything else that makes you feel comfortable. Do whatever you can to become even more immersed in the current moment. You may choose to diffuse essential oils, brew yourself a luxurious beverage, turn on some of your favorite music, or do any other number of things that will make the experience more peaceful and comforting. These activities will also help draw your awareness to the present situation, making it even more enjoyable for you.

The more you associate your home with peace, comfort, and calmness, the easier it will be to remain mindful when you are home. This is important because you want your home to be a space that is comfortable and safe for you. You should not feel like you have to compensate for difficult emotions or situations when you are in your home. Instead, it should feel like a sanctuary that allows you the opportunity to relieve yourself of the stressors of the external world, and truly enjoy your present moment.

There are many times that you can practice being mindfulness in practical applications. For some people, these opportunities for practicing mindfulness are the best ones, because they allow you to be the most present without having to go out of your way to do so. You do not have to use prompts or "sit on the sidelines" for any given period of time to be mindful. Instead, you simply allow yourself the chance to become mindful at routine moments and turn it into an enjoyable practice that you look forward to on a daily basis. It should be a chance to regroup and recover from anything that may be drawing your attention out and causing stress in your daily life.

Chapter 5: Maintaining Mindfulness

Mindfulness is something that we must practice, constantly. It is not something we achieve ones and maintain forever. Rather, it is something that we must practice on a daily basis in order to maintain. Knowing this, you may find it sometimes is harder to maintain your state of mindfulness than it is for other times. Allow this to bring you peace, knowing that falling out of tune is completely normal. Additionally, the more you fall out of tune and regain your mindfulness, the easier it will be to regain it in the future.

Sometimes, it may be days or even weeks before you notice that you have fallen out of the routine of mindfulness. When you are brand new to the practice, it is easy to forget that you are working to be more mindful in your life. It is not uncommon for people to be extremely mindful for the first several days, and then just completely forget about it. Or, they may even become worn out. Sometimes, being mindful really forces us to confront emotional triggers that we are not interested in confronting. This can make it feel difficult to maintain and may make you feel like it is more comfortable to be ignorant than it is to be mindful. Realize that it is completely normal to run into these blocks, even for the most mindful people you will ever meet.

There are many ways you can contribute to maintaining your mindfulness, several of which we have already explored and discussed in this book. However, it is important to realize that it won't always be easy to maintain your mindfulness. As you've already learned, when there is chaos or confrontation, or when you are experiencing pandemonium, it can be difficult to maintain your mindfulness.

However, sometimes it's just difficult in general. When you are not already wired to a mindful state, it can be hard to remember to stay mindful. Sometimes, you might struggle to remember to do it, not just during hard times, but at any time, because you are not used to it. You may find that you don't realize you haven't been mindful until after the situation has already passed, and then feel guilty or regretful that you didn't do it differently.

There are several things you should realize and do if this occurs, which will help you maintain a mindful state, even if it's sometimes difficult to remember. Below, we are going to explore the various stages of regaining mindfulness, even when you are forgetful or hardwired to respond to situations in a different way.

Give Yourself Permission to Go Slow

Changes don't happen overnight, especially when you are talking about changes for things that you have been doing for many years, perhaps even your whole life. There are no magic formulas, genies or spells that you can use to help you instantaneously become a more mindful person. Instead, you will have to work towards being mindful every day of your life, even once you've already mastered the art of mindfulness.

It is important that you give yourself permission to go as slow as you need to. You are not going to be able to respond to every single situation with mindfulness just because you've decided that's what you want to do. Instead, you are going to find that you will actually rarely respond with mindfulness at first, and that may be very frustrating for you. Realize that you will need to take your time and respect your need to go slow and take this as a learning process. The changes that last the longest are the ones that can take the longest to create. The more effort you have to put in to get yourself into a changed state of mind, the more likely that state will last you. Even if you have to maintain it.

It may take you several weeks, maybe even months to become mindful. Some people even take years to master it. You never know how long it will take you, because of all of the different elements that go into being mindful. Your unique blocks and resistances, lifestyle, and existing level of mindfulness, plus many other things will all contribute to how quickly you can become mindful the majority of the time.

Start Recognizing Triggers

The very first step to switching over to *mindfulness* as your new full-time lifestyle is recognizing triggers. If you are having a hard time maintaining your mindfulness practice because of forgetfulness or a later realization that you "could have" responded with mindfulness, it may be because you are not recognizing your triggers. Take some time and start realizing what your triggers are. These will change on a regular basis, just like life does, so you will need to consistently maintain a check-in process where you recognize what your triggers are and learn why they cause you to respond in certain ways. The more you understand this, the easier it will be for you to maintain mindfulness.

It is not beneficial to judge your triggers. Doing this can cause you to create new blocks and resistances which may further drive you away from a mindful state. Instead, you simply want to recognize what they are. This is an opportunity for you to look deeper within yourself and work on it. At first, there is nothing more that you need to do other than to simply recognize these triggers. Remember, changes don't happen overnight. Instead, you are going to need to take your time. Once you recognize these triggers, practice recognizing them in action. Every time a trigger of yours occurs, recognize it has happened and allow yourself to experience it. Don't encourage any changes yet, just recognize these triggers in action. You will need to practice recognizing new triggers every time one occurs in your life, which is why it is such an important step in maintaining your mindfulness practice.

Create Your Ideal Response

Once you recognize your new triggers and are very confident in your ability to become mindful about them as they are actively happening, you are ready to create your ideal response. You may have already been thinking of an ideal response up until now, but now is the time to think of a practical, mindful and realistic response that you could use when these triggers arise. This should represent your ideal method of how you would want to respond to a trigger.

For example, let's imagine that a particular person makes you angry when you are speaking to them. It gets to the point that you no longer have to hear anything from them at all for you to become angry. Rather, you just become angry from seeing them in general! In this instance, it may seem like the person is the trigger. However, it is likely something that this person has done, said or expressed in the past that has created the trigger. This, in turn, led to a situation where every time you see this person, you think about that experience.

Your ideal response may be that every time you see this person, you feel no emotions at all. You don't necessarily need to feel good or better when you see them. You just need to eliminate the uncomfortable and charged emotions, like anger and hurt. Knowing this, you may set the intention that every time you see this person, you will no longer feel emotionally charged. Instead, you will just feel neutral.

The above situation and correlating ideal response system can be applied to virtually any trigger you experience in life. Once you recognize the trigger and understand when it is actively happening, you'll likely start gaining more information about *why* it happens when you are in that specific situation. Knowing that, you can create an ideal response on how you would rather feel and respond to the situation, versus how you are actively responding. Make sure that the ideal response is something realistic and achievable. Setting the bar too high may prevent you from achieving it at all.

Use Your Ideal Response at Least 25% Of The Time

Again, you need to be prepared to move slowly. You cannot expect that just because you have recognized the trigger and set the intention that you will now respond perfectly every single time. That in itself just isn't realistic. Instead, you should be prepared to respond your ideal way at least 25% of the time. This allows you the opportunity to prepare to respond that way, but also gives you immediate permission that if the situation doesn't go as you desire for it to go, it won't be a "failure" on your part. Rather, it is just one of the 75% of instances where mindfulness hasn't taken root yet!

When you notice the trigger, think about your ideal response. The first several times, you may only think about the response and how you may have made it work in that situation. Eventually, you will arrive at a situation where the ideal response feels like it naturally wants to take place from you. This is the time where you can start practicing it. The more you practice it, the easier it will become for you.

It is important to understand that this is a major part of maintaining mindfulness. Sometimes, you may put in all of the effort to eliminate a trigger, only for it to come back again. If you notice a trigger has fully come back to you, you will need to revert back to this step and practice integrating your ideal response. You may even need to adjust your ideal response to be something more appropriate and fitting so that it is easier for you to respond to it.

Realize that this part of the process takes a long time. It may even take you a long time just to get to the 25% mark. Again, give yourself the chance to take as much time as you need, and don't hold judgment for yourself or the situation when you need time. Giving yourself this permission is the best way to make sure that you don't feel as though you are failing, and that you allow yourself to respond in the most comfortable way. Believe it or not, the more you take the pressure off of yourself to act a certain way, the easier it will be for you to act the way you actually want to act. Eventually, it will come extremely naturally.

Practice the 80/20 Rule

Moving to the 80/20 rule is sometimes gradual, but you should keep this rule in mind as your destination point. While it will be difficult to get here right away, eventually this is where you should aim to end up. It is natural that we may experience triggers, even long after we have worked through them and moved on. Sometimes, it's just something that happens. If you can stay mindful at least 80 percent of the time, then you are doing well. More, and you are golden!

Having a rule like the 80/20 rule gives you permission to make mistakes, without having to consider that as a complete failure of your mindfulness practice. It can take off a great deal of stress and pressure, and make it even easier to be mindful the majority of the time. This works even better because it makes you mindful about your mindfulness. That way, on the times you make a mistake, rather than beating yourself up you can take a look at *why* the trigger happened again, and address it. This will give you the best chance of making sure that you can eliminate triggers once and for all.

Watch Deep Rooted Changes Take Place

The longer you practice mindfulness, the deeper it will root itself in your life. Eventually, you will always address things in this method: by recognizing a trigger, addressing it, creating an alternative response, and enforcing that response at least most of the time. Over time, this will be a natural method for you to address virtually everything in your life, and that will ultimately shift you from a life of ignorance towards your troubles and into a life of mindfulness.

Mindfulness is not an overnight practice that can be mastered right away. Instead, you will have to practice and maintain your practice for the rest of your life. It will become much easier in time, but even when you are a master at mindfulness, you may still find there will be times where you struggle to be mindful.

This is because life is ever-changing and we are emotionally charged beings that will sometimes react instead of respond.

However, you will notice in time that many deep-rooted and powerful changes take place in your life that will guide you in the direction of mindfulness. As this practice becomes more natural to you, you will realize that you are mindful at least 80% of the time in your entire life. You may not notice the changes as they are occurring, but one day you will look back and see just how far you have come!

Always Journal About It

If you are not one to recognize changes that happen in your own life, a good way to start recognizing them is to journal about it. The more you journal about your experiences, the more you can analyze them and make changes, as well as see how far you have come. Journaling has many great purposes when it comes to maintaining your mindfulness practice.

First off, when you journal you can truly gain a greater insight as to how far you have come. You will start to see exactly where you were when you started, and where you are now. You will likely notice that your ability to make changes become quicker and quicker the longer that you practice your mindfulness strategies, and also that you are more capable of adapting to harder situations.

Additionally, journaling is a great way to identify triggers, understand your blocks, and really gain a deeper insight as to what you are going through. Then, you can make more mindful and realistic approaches to how you will handle the situation and what you will do about it. Sometimes, writing about it can significantly help you alleviate a good portion of the stress that is associated with any given situation. As well, you may notice certain trends that occur in regards to your triggers or emotions and have a greater idea as to how you can increase the peace and positivity in your life through your mindfulness practices.

Journaling is an important part of making major life changes. It allows you to reflect deeper on what you are going through, track your progress, and empty yourself of many thoughts that may be using up extra space in your mind. Then, you can focus on the positive and powerful things you want to focus on, and you don't have to keep them in your mind taking up valuable real estate.

Respect, Love, and Honor Yourself Anyway

Some people who are practicing mindfulness may find it difficult to keep themselves positive and love themselves through the struggles. This is especially true when triggers are particularly emotional, or for those who are really early into their mindfulness practice. It can be easy to feel like you are failing, doing something wrong, or otherwise not having success in your practice. You may also find it easy to punish yourself or drag yourself down for what you are going through. It is important to realize that this is not beneficial and that it can actually detract from your mindfulness practice.

A major part of being mindful is feeling positive about yourself and your life. While this may not come easily to you, it is something you should focus on working towards. If you struggle with mindfulness for these reasons, one of your first missions should be to identify your triggers that get you feeling down on yourself and work through those first. You need to learn to practice respecting, loving and honoring yourself anyway.

There is nothing more detrimental to your mindfulness practice than being out of love and harmony with yourself. This can cause you to sabotage your ability to be mindful because you will tear yourself down every time you make a mistake. That is why it is crucial to give yourself room to make mistakes and to love yourself anyway. The easier you are on yourself and the less you hold yourself in contempt for your mistakes, the easier it will be for you to practice mindfulness in your life. It is very important that you give yourself space and permission to make mistakes, and that you love yourself anyway. This will allow you to be the most successful you can possibly be in your mindfulness practice.

As you can see, it won't always be easy to be mindful. Especially when you are brand new to the practice. Sometimes, it won't necessarily be chaos or difficult times that make it hard for you to be mindful. Sometimes, you will simply have a hard time remembering to practice this new way of life due to you being used to living life in a different way for so long. The best thing you can do is give yourself time and space, and draw yourself back to your practice whenever you realize you've strayed away. It may take a while to get there, but the more you practice, the more naturally it will come to you and the more successful you will be in your mindfulness.

Conclusion

Mindfulness is a powerful practice that has the ability to change your life in incredible ways. When you are mindful, you may experience better health, better emotional balances, and lower stress levels. You will give yourself the opportunity to relieve yourself from symptoms of stress. You also gain the ability to recognize what causes you discomfort, and practice working through it so that you can avoid experiencing those unpleasant experiences in the future. Of course, conflict cannot be eliminated, but you allow yourself to grow as a person and work through these conflicts more easily.

The practice of mindfulness can be done anywhere: in your car, at work, at home, or even when you're standing in line at the grocery store. You do not have to limit your practice to any one place or experience. As well, you do not need several minutes or hours to devote to a practice of mindfulness. Instead, you can practice it in as little as two minutes, if that is all you have to dedicate. In fact, it is better to practice mindfulness for a short period of times several times over the course of the day than it is to practice one long burst and never do it again for the rest of the day.

I hope that you learned how to use mindfulness in your daily habits and that it will greatly help you in achieving a more peaceful and empowered life. The practical methods in this book were shared in order to teach you how mindfulness works and exactly how you can work it into your busy routine.

If you enjoyed this book, I ask that you please take the time to rate it on Amazon Kindle. Your honest review would be greatly appreciated.

Thank you, and enjoy your mindful life!

Help me improve this book

While I have never met you, if you made it through this book I know that you are the kind of person that is wanting to get better and is willing to take on tough feedback to get to that point. You and I are cut from the same cloth in that respect. I am always looking to get better and I wish to not just improve myself, but also this book. If you have positive feedback, please take the time to leave a review. It will help other find this book and it can help change a life in the same way that it changed yours. If you have constructive feedback, please also leave a review. It will help me better understand what you, the reader, need to make significant improvements in your life. I will take your feedback and use it to improve this book so that it can become more powerful and beneficial to all those who encounter it.

REMEMBER TO JOIN THE GROUP NOW!

If you have not joined the Mastermind Self Development group yet, now is your time! You will receive videos and articles from top authorities in self development as well as a special group only offers on new books and training programs. There will also be a monthly member only draw that gives you a chance to win any book from your Kindle wish list!

If you sign up through this link http://www.mastermindselfdevelopment.com/specialreport you will also get a special free report on the Wheel of Life. This report will give you a visual look at your current life and then take you through a series of exercises that will help you plan what your perfect life looks like. The workbook does not end there; we then take you through a process to help you plan how to achieve that perfect life. The process is very powerful and has the potential to change your life forever. Join the group now and start to change your life!
http://www.mastermindselfdevelopment.com/specialreport

You will also love these other great titles from Mastermind Self Development!

You will want to check out these other great titles Mastermind Self Development. All available in the Kindle store or you can just click on covers below.

getBook.at/learnfrench   myBook.to/learnspanish

getBook.at/learnlanguages   viewBook.at/selflove

You can also find these titles by searching them in the Kindle store on Amazon.

Mindfulness for Beginners

Secrets to Getting Rid of Stress and Staying in the Moment

Free membership into the Mastermind Self Development Group!

For a limited time, you can join the Mastermind Self Development Group for free! You will receive videos and articles from top authorities in self development as well as a special group only offers on new books and training programs. There will also be a monthly member only draw that gives you a chance to win any book from your Kindle wish list!

If you sign up through this link http://www.mastermindselfdevelopment.com/specialreport you will also get a special free report on the Wheel of Life. This report will give you a visual look at your current life and then take you through a series of exercises that will help you plan what your perfect life looks like. The workbook does not end there; we then take you through a process to help you plan how to achieve that perfect life. The process is very powerful and has the potential to change your life forever. Join the group now and start to change your life!
http://www.mastermindselfdevelopment.com/specialreport

© Copyright 2017 By Mastermind Self Development All rights reserved.

This document is geared towards providing exact and reliable information in regards to the topic and issue covered. The publication is sold with the idea that the publisher is not required to render accounting, officially permitted, or otherwise, qualified services. If advice is necessary, legal or professional, a practiced individual in the profession should be ordered.

From a Declaration of Principles which was accepted and approved equally by a Committee of the American Bar Association and a Committee of Publishers and Associations.

In no way is it legal to reproduce, duplicate, or transmit any part of this document in either electronic means or in printed format. Recording of this publication is strictly prohibited and any storage of this document is not allowed unless with written permission from the publisher. All rights reserved.

The information provided herein is stated to be truthful and consistent, in that any liability, in terms of inattention or otherwise, by any usage or abuse of any policies, processes, or directions contained within is the solitary and utter responsibility of the recipient reader. Under no circumstances will any legal responsibility or blame be held against the publisher for any reparation, damages, or monetary loss due to the information herein, either directly or indirectly.

Respective authors own all copyrights not held by the publisher.

The information herein is offered for informational purposes solely, and is universal as so. The presentation of the information is without contract or any type of guarantee assurance.

The trademarks that are used are without any consent, and the publication of the trademark is without permission or backing by the trademark owner. All trademarks and brands within this book are for clarifying purposes only and are the owned by the owners themselves, not affiliated with this document.

Table of Contents

Introduction

Chapter 1: The Secret

Chapter 2: Eliminating Stress

Chapter 3: Staying in the Moment

Chapter 4: Easy Application

Chapter 5: Mindfulness Mastery

Conclusion

Introduction

Mindfulness is a powerful practice that can help you transform your life using simple strategies. Although it may seem difficult at first, mindfulness practices can help you take action in eliminating the stress in your life and staying in the moment. When you practice mindfulness, you learn a great deal about self-awareness and personal care. Mindfulness practices are an excellent tool in learning to navigate your inner self and develop a life that is more peaceful and enjoyable.

In this book *Mindfulness for Beginners: Secrets to Getting Rid of Stress and Staying in the Moment*, you are going to learn a series of valuable and practical applications of mindfulness to help you along your journey. This book is specially designed for anyone who is looking to develop a mindfulness practice but who may not have any clue as to where to start. You will learn about what mindfulness is and isn't, why it is so important to have a mindfulness practice, and easy ways you can develop your own.

Whether you have never heard of mindfulness before or you have dabbled in the practices here and there, this book will help you get on track to lead a more stress-free and positive life. Each chapter is created to provide you with the best and most accurate information to help you along your unique journey and create a practice that will help you eliminate your own personal stresses. To get the maximum benefit from this book, please read it at your own pace, the one that feels most comfortable for you. Enjoy.

Chapter 1: The Secret

Many people think mindfulness is a practice only used by religious groups who have several hours a day to meditate and explore their inner selves. The reality is, mindfulness is actually a phenomenal practice that can be used by anyone to create a more stress-free life. People who are mindful have an easier time staying in the moment, are better at letting things roll off their back, and are more likely to have a more positive and peaceful life with a healthier mental and emotional state.

There are many secrets to mastering mindfulness, but first, you are going to learn exactly what mindfulness is and what it isn't.

Mindfulness Is…

Mindfulness is a practice whereby people learn to tune into their inner selves and identify feelings and emotions they experience in relation to internal and external influences. When people learn to tune into themselves, they gain greater insight into who they are, what they are, and how they are. They learn which things make them feel certain ways and the best coping methods for their unique personality type. Since each person is so vastly different from another, mindfulness is a deeply personal practice that will be experienced entirely different from person to person. Although the methods to develop a mindfulness practice and achieve mindfulness states are similar between each person, the ways people act and react to the experiences, emotions, and feelings that arise for them are completely different.

You can witness mindfulness in yourself when you have an experience, and your first reaction is to look into yourself and identify what you are experiencing in relation to your circumstances. For example, say a co-worker takes credit for the work you did, and instead of fighting, the first thing you do is look inside yourself and see what you feel and how you feel. Once you identify these feelings, you take action based on what feels right for you. When experiences are handled in this manner, they are handled in a way that is optimal to everyone involved. If you were to fight, you would likely not accomplish anything other than to show your boss that you tend to get emotionally charged in these situations. You may experience further frustration and embarrassment or other uncomfortable feelings as a result of your reaction. However, if you were to first look inside and identify your emotions and feelings and then approach the situation in a calmer approach based on what felt right for you, the situation would be handled much easier. Your boss would see how calm and collected you were, you would feel much better knowing that you handled the situation with dignity, and the person who lied would not be a greater cause of stress or frustration for you because you would not actively be in an argument with them.

There are many practical situations in life where you would want to have a mindfulness practice on your side. Many of the experiences we have in life we react to without realizing we have reacted. We then experience the aftershocks of the experience, and many times, they can have negative effects on us. When we have a mindfulness practice in place, we are more likely to recognize the situations that trigger these experiences and identify the ways that we can eliminate our reactions to the triggers. Then, we can choose new preferred methods of responding to the situation and adjust our responses to our desired method. After a while of responding instead of reacting, your reaction will change to your desired response. Then, it will feel natural for you to respond in the way that feels better to you and serves you better.

Mindfulness is a practice that assists people in exploring their inner self and the way they experience the world around them. It is a system of strategies that help you develop a mental state that can assist you in identifying who you are, how you respond to the world, and what makes you feel good. When you learn these things, you gain greater control over your life and your emotions as you learn how you can effectively interact with the world in a way that brings you joy and happiness.

Mindfulness Is Not…

Mindfulness is a powerful practice to help you identify triggers and switch up your response method so that you feel better about the way you lead your life. It is not a magic tool that erases triggers and rewrites your reality without any of your assistance. Think of mindfulness as a pencil with an eraser at one end. Using your own guidance, you and the pencil can work together to erase things you dislike. The marks are left on the page, but they fade away. Then, using your guidance, you and the pencil can rewrite something new into that space. Still, the marks remain beneath the new words, but the new words are more prominent and visible as opposed to the old ones. The old ones are no longer important and no longer hold the priority on the page. Now, everything is focused on the new reality that is written onto the page.

Mindfulness is just like a pencil in a way that it is a tool you can use to erase things you dislike and rewrite your reality. Mindfulness is not a magic wand that will erase your reality and rewrite it for you however, without any effort on your behalf. If you do not put effort into your mindfulness practice, it will not thrive and you will not see the benefits from it. You need to realize that mindfulness is not a medicine, antidote, or magical eraser for life. You will still remember the triggers and you will still identify them even long after they have been rewritten; however, they will not affect you in the same way. They will not be as prominent as they once were. Instead, the prominent experience will be your new reality that you have consciously created using mindfulness as a tool and your own efforts as the driving force.

The Secret

The secret to mindfulness is really simple. So simple in fact, that you might think it's not even a secret at all, nor is it all that impressive. The reality is, when you understand this secret and you put it into effect, your mindfulness practice will grow exponentially, and you will reap in all of the benefits that mindfulness has to offer. The secret to mindfulness is to practice regularly. Mindfulness is not something you attain and then never have to work for again. Mindfulness is called a "practice" for a reason. You must practice each day and put in effort to see the results from your practice. The more you put into your practice, the more you will get out.

That being said, you should not feel like you have to practice mindfulness 24/7. Instead, mindfulness should be regarded as a tool that you use when it is needed, to help you lead a more stress-free and positive lifestyle. Whenever you notice you are feeling overwhelmed, unhappy, stressed, frustrated, or otherwise uncomfortable, you can use mindfulness to help you work through those feelings. If you feel as though you are distracted or have left, mindfulness is a great practice to help bring you back into the room and experience life for what it is.

When you learn about the value of mindfulness and start seeing the results in your own life, you will understand how powerful this practice truly is. The more you use it, the more results you will see, and the more you will remember to use it. In the beginning, you may discover that it is hard to be mindful in many of the situations you encounter. This is completely natural, and you will eventually learn to be mindful more frequently. The best thing you can do is remember that mindfulness takes practice and it isn't a magic wand that can solve all of your problems. It is, however, a tool that you can use when necessary to regain control over your life and reduce the amount of stress you experience.

Chapter 2: Eliminating Stress

One of the best benefits of using mindfulness practices is eliminating stress from your life. While it can take some time, especially if stress is embedded in many areas of your life, the more you practice mindfulness, the easier it will be for you to eliminate the impact that stress has on your life. You will never completely remove stress from your life, but you will be able to alter the way it affects you and how you choose to respond to stress. You can choose to see stress as the end-all-be-all that turns your life upside down, or you can use it as a trigger that informs you that you need to be mindful and change your ways.

There are many techniques you can use to reduce and eliminate stress in your life using mindfulness strategies. The way you choose to do this practice will be entirely up to you and what feels right for you. Generally, most people follow a similar outline but use different specific practices to help them eliminate the stress. The reason why there are so many unique practices is because the way people respond, react, and cope towards different things varies. It is important that you choose practices that resonate well with you, as these are what will carry the highest impact with your results.

Step 1: Identification

The first step to being mindful around stress is identifying the stress. Once you realize you are stressed out, even if you're just slightly stressed, you can start to uncover what is causing that stress. After you recognize the stress, you want to start identifying where it is affecting your life. If it is a large amount of stress, it may be affecting your life in many ways. It could affect the way you sleep, socialize, eat, and take care of yourself. If it is a smaller amount of stress, it may be a little harder to detect where it is affecting your life. Still, stress always affects us in one way or another, so identify all of the ways you are being affected by it.

Realizing you are stressed and identifying the symptoms are the first major key in making sure that you are being mindful around the stress. You have already become mindful of its existence and the impact it has on your life. The next step is to identify where the stress is coming from. Some people recognize the trigger immediately, but others do not. It may be possible for you to think your stress is coming from one area when in reality it is coming from somewhere else. For example, you may think you are stressed out from work, but the real problem is you're not resting enough so you're stressed from being too tired. Once you identify the true culprit of the stress, you can start making changes to eliminate the stress.

Step 2: Eliminating the Stress

This process can be more difficult, especially if the source of your stress is large or carries a heavy emotional value for you. It is extremely important however, as this is the process where all of your results will come from. Later in this book, you will learn about easy and practical applications for mindfulness practices, but for now, you simply need to understand the goal.

The goal in this step is to get into the cause of the stress and eliminate it. Much like picking a weed from a garden, you need to eliminate it from the roots. If you eliminate it only from the base and not the roots, then you are going to find that it will come back in the future, and it may even come back worse. You need to resolve the issue entirely so that it is no longer a problem for you. This can be extremely hard. Once again, if the cause of the stress holds a high emotional value for you, you may struggle to work through it. Some things you can do to make it easier include journaling, getting support, and asking for help. You may not always be able to do it on your own, and having advice and support from others can be extremely helpful.

For some issues, eliminating the stress will take as little as one or two actions. For others, it may take weeks of efforts and practice before you eliminate it. You may even fail a few times at eliminating it before it resolves entirely. The most important thing is that you keep working at it until the issue is no longer present for you. As you start working through it more and more and you start feeling the benefits of the outcome, you will likely find that it is much easier for you to continue working because of that. Soon enough, the issue will be resolved entirely, and you will be able to move on from the ailment.

Step 3: Releasing the Rest

Eliminating the stress can be stressful in itself, and you want to make sure that you release anything that comes up throughout this process. Especially when we have high emotional attachment to certain situations, it can stir up a lot of emotions that need to be worked through. The mindful approach is to recognize these emotions and practice releasing them in a healthy way. Once you do, you will feel definitely better, and you will see that the more you release, the easier everything feels in the long run.

Step 4: Create Healthy New Habits

Once you eliminate a stress and release the emotions around the elimination process, you can identify a new habit you want to implement and start using it. Using the previous example, if you are stressed due to a lack of rest, you may wish to start going to bed earlier or eliminate distractions from the bedroom to make falling asleep easier. Identifying the healthy replacement habits might be easy, or it might be difficult. If the habit seems new and daunting to you, you may wish to start implementing it slowly so that it's easier for you to adopt into your lifestyle. When you are choosing healthy new habits, choose ones that are realistic to you. If you choose new habits that have no emotional value to you, you are likely not going to keep them for long, and you will revert back to old patterns. For example, if you are someone who dislikes running and doesn't have a strong desire to start but you try to implement a new routine to run every evening to help tire you out because you heard it would help, you likely won't keep the habit for long. Instead, you want to pick something that is going to be comfortable for you and make it easy for you to practice in your daily life. The new healthy habit needs to be enjoyable and reasonable so that it lasts, and you do not end up reverting back to unhealthy patterns and recreating stress in your life again. If you find yourself slipping back into old patterns, identify the triggers causing the slip and make necessary changes to keep yourself from regressing.

Step 5: Maintenance

After all is said and done, you will want to maintain your mindfulness practice around stress. Complete the above steps any time you notice stress in your life, no matter how big or small the stress is. If you choose coping methods that do not seem to be working for you, try and discover why and then choose new ones that work better. Part of the mindfulness practice is exploring what works and doesn't work for you and understanding why. When you do this, you learn more about yourself and create the perfect environment for you to continue down your mindfulness journey. Think of this as a working relationship where you will always have to put effort into mindfulness and into learning more about yourself. The more you learn and grow, however, the deeper the connection comes and the easier it is to navigate the journey even during harder times.

Mindfulness has a powerful ability to help eliminate stress and make life a lot easier to manage. It may be difficult to use mindfulness around stress at first, especially if you have a lot of it your life. Start by identifying the largest source of stress and then work your way down from there. With some time, effort, and maintenance, you will find yourself leading a stress-free life thanks to your mindfulness practices. Remember, just because you are being mindful doesn't mean stress won't arise. It simply means that your approach to stress will be altered, and therefore, it will not affect you on the same level that it once did. Instead of infesting your life and ruling it, it will simply be recognized as a trigger to make some changes and start honoring yourself and your needs in a new way.

You are halfway done!

Congratulations on making it to the halfway point of the journey. Many try and give up long before even getting to this point, so you are to be congratulated on this. You have shown that you are serious about getting better every day. I am also serious about improving my life, and helping others get better along the way. To do this I need your feedback. Click on the link below and take a moment to let me know how this book has helped you. If you feel there is something missing or something you would like to see differently, I would love to know about it. I want to ensure that as you and I improve, this book continues to improve as well. Thank you for taking the time to ensure that we are all getting the most from each other.

Chapter 3: Staying in the Moment

Staying in the moment is one of the best ways to enjoy life to its fullest. When you stay in the moment, you experience everything that every moment has to offer. You give yourself the best opportunity to really absorb the joy that comes with life, as well as understand every lesson and experience that is sent your way. Sometimes, especially when the moment is painful or stress is present, staying in the moment can be really difficult. Other times, we are so used to being away from the moment that we struggle to stay in the moment at all. There are many wonderful practices you can use to stay in the moment. Again, which practices you use will greatly depend on what kind of personality you have and what you prefer. In the next chapter, you will learn about practical mindfulness applications.

Using mindfulness as a guide to stay in the moment is a great strategy. The general outline for how you use mindfulness for this purpose is the same for most people, it is merely the practices that change from person to person. When you want to stay mindful of each moment, the following steps will help you with the process.

Step 1: Identify When You Leave the Moment

The first step to staying in the moment is identifying the minute you left the moment. The second you stop being in the moment is exactly what you need to identify. Once you do, you will find it significantly easier for you to make the necessary changes. Identifying the moment can be hard, as it may happen when you aren't paying attention. If you are so used to leaving that it comes naturally to you, you may check about the very fact that you have left. This can make the entire process a lot more difficult. If this is true for you, the simple fact of realizing that you have left helps significantly. For others, you may already be well aware of when or why you have left.

Something to consider is that when a situation is emotionally charged, we often leave because we want to protect ourselves from the situation. We do not want to experience the painful emotions, so we leave as a means to shield ourselves from what we believe is coming next. If you are in a situation where you are leaving because of emotions, there are two things you need to think about. First, these are the situations you need to do work around. These are the ones where you need to identify what is causing you to leave and how you can make changes so that you can stay in the moment. Second, you need to stay because there is a valuable lesson to be learned and you won't learn it by leaving. When you are ready, get back in and experience the lesson.

If you are unaware of when or why you are leaving or there doesn't seem to be a specific cause, then simply realizing that you have left is enough. Realize when you have left, and affirm to yourself that you have done so. Then, move on to step two.

Step 2: Be within Yourself

Before you are back into the situation, you need to be within yourself. If something has caused you to leave, what is it? Why are you leaving? What is making you feel the need to go inwards or mentally remove yourself from the situation? Try and identify as much around the situation as possible. Sometimes, the answer may simply be that you were bored. Other times, there may be a more complex or painful answer. The most important thing is that you take the time to identify the answer. Then, you can figure out what to do about it.

Regardless of why you left, take a minute to recognize what actions you took when you left. Did you start thinking about other things? Did you stop listening to the people around you? Did you pick up your phone and start blankly scrolling news feeds or otherwise showing that you were not present in the moment? Take the time to identify what your patterns and behaviors are when you leave the moment. These are the patterns and behaviors that you are going to want to use to your advantage, as they will become your triggers to help you recognize when you have left in the future.

Step 3: Be Present

By now, you should be aware that you left, maybe have a reason as to why, and have a clear idea of what you do when you leave. Now, you can practice becoming present. If you are completely away, take your time and start bringing yourself back into the moment. You can use any number of the practices described in the next chapter, as long as the outcome is that you feel more present in the moment. The majority of the process will be based on grounding. If there is a negative or uncomfortable emotional value to the situation, you may want to take note of that so you can deal with it now or at a more reasonable time.

As you stay in the moment, let yourself start to experience everything more fully. When distracting thoughts or feelings of getting out come around, simply let them roll off your back and do what you can to stay focused in the moment. It can take time to master this process, but soon enough, you will be able to easily get back in when you have left.

Step 4: Maintenance

As with other mindfulness practices, there is a maintenance that needs to be done to ensure that you stay more frequently. If you are brand new to being in the moment, you will likely struggle to stay for long periods of time. The most important thing is that you do not go hard on yourself. Give yourself space and time to adjust to the new practices and let yourself get used to the idea. Whenever you recognize you're not being present, simply regather your focus and get back in the moment again. The more you become practiced with this, the easier it will be.

Being present in the moment is another working relationship. You will not always be present in the moment, no matter how developed your mindfulness practices are. When you are experiencing high emotions or are having stress in your life, which you will, you will likely leave a lot more frequently. The mindful approach is to recognize when you are leaving and if there is an emotional value to the reason why, such as stress or grief, you do what you can to eliminate the root of the problem and resolve the issues. Then, you can carry on with your mindfulness practice and staying in the moment.

Mindfulness is the best way to stay present in the moment. Being present in the moment is one of the major purposes behind mindfulness practices. When you are present in the moment, whether the moment feels good or not, you gain so much more from it. You learn lessons about yourself, you experience things more deeply, and you open yourself up to a greater opportunity to experience joy. Even the moments that don't feel good are valuable. You learn about how they make you feel, the triggers that you have, and the things that you can do to work through those triggers in a way that feels good for you.

Chapter 4: Easy Application

Mindfulness practices vary based on what you need from your practice, but ultimately, they all have the same goal: to help you achieve a mindful state. These practices are easy to apply in your life, and they are extremely practical. You do not need to set aside several minutes or hours in a day to complete these tasks. In fact, if you do not desire, you don't even need to have a scheduled time in the day where you practice mindfulness. Though, it is recommended. The most important thing is that the techniques you use are ones that feel good to you and help you achieve the primary goal: to become mindful.

Grounding Techniques

When you are feeling particularly overwhelmed with emotions or you find that you are struggling to stay present in the moment, grounding techniques are very powerful. They can help get you out of your head and bring you back into the present and address situations with a more mindful and tactful approach.

5, 4, 3, 2, 1!

Perhaps one of the most popular grounding methods is the 5, 4, 3, 2, 1 method. This method is quite simple and allows you to identify your surroundings quickly and stay more focused on them. You can complete it by first identifying five things that you see, and then four things that you can feel (physically). Then, you can identify three things you hear, two things you smell, and one thing you taste. Take your time as you work through each step and really let yourself experience the process. The point is to absorb more of your surroundings and release your dominant thoughts. Doing so will make it much easier for you to come back into the present moment and stay aware of your real life situation. This is a great technique for any situation where grounding might be needed. You can do it quietly in your head or say it out loud if you feel comfortable doing so in your given situation.

Light Beams

Another great grounding technique is to imagine that you are being pierced by a light beam. The beam should start in the sun and work its way through the top of your head and down your spine. Then, it will come out the bottom of your tail bone and connect into the center of the Earth. When you imagine this light beam, it helps you remember that you are connected to everything and we are one. There is nothing that separates you from the Earth, nor the sun or anything else. If you are feeling an overwhelming amount of emotions, you may wish to imagine the light beam carrying them away and releasing them into the Earth to be eliminated completely.

Firm Roots

Some people prefer to use roots as their grounding technique. Instead of imagining a light beam, they choose to imagine that there are roots under their feet that are firmly connecting them to the ground. These roots are planted in the Earth, and they cannot possibly be separated from it any easier than a massive tree could be. You can imagine yourself developing roots by first taking a deep breathing into your diaphragm and then filling your lungs. As you breathe it out, imagine roots growing from the bottom of your feet and into the Earth beneath you. Feel your feet firmly planted on the ground and recognize that you are connected to the Earth, and there is nothing that can take you away from that.

Triggered Practices

When you are feeling triggered by a particular situation or subject, you will want to use a mindfulness practice to help you through the situation. When you are mindful in triggered situations, you have greater control over yourself. You eliminate reactions and increase your ability to respond in a way that feels comfortable and appropriate for you. This gives you greater control over yourself in the situation, which can allow you to gain virtually anything you want from it. You cannot control the situation you are in, but you can control how it impacts you.

Recognize, Analyze, and Release

Perhaps the best way to respond to a triggered event is to practice the recognize, analyze, and release method. This essentially means that you recognize you have been triggered, analyze everything that comes up with the trigger, and then release it. When you are analyzing the trigger, you will want to see what caused you to feel a certain way, as well as the emotions and feelings that came up when you did feel that way. You should also take the time to analyze anything else that may arise in your personal situation as you are analyzing the situation. Then, once you are aware of everything, release it. If you need to, you can keep track of things that really stood out to you and work on them when you have the time to do releasing methods. If you have the time right away, then of course you should do it. However, if you still have to do things and are not in a space where you can take a few minutes to yourself, simply imagine that, as you breathe out, the issue is exhaled as well and you are released from the feelings, emotions, and thoughts until you are ready to revisit them. It is imperative that you revisit them soon, within 24 hours if possible. This will prevent them from becoming suppressed and turning into a larger problem.

Take Five

When you are triggered by something and you have a bit of time, spending time on the trigger is a good idea. Take a short break if you can, such as by heading outside, to the bathroom, or to another quiet place. When you are there, take a few deep breaths and visualize the experience the moment you were triggered. What did it feel like? What was your initial reaction? Similar to recognize, analyze, and release, ask yourself questions that will help you identify the situation and how it made you feel inside. As you do, take the time to really pay attention to everything. Even take the time to pay attention to your present thoughts and feelings as you continue to analyze the situation. Once you are aware, you can spend the last part of your break doing deep belly breaths. These are a great release mechanism that can help you bring yourself back to the center and feel more at peace as you get back to your day. If you find that there are prominent feelings or stressors that are still present after your break, you should take time to revisit these when you have enough time to sit and focus on them for a while.

Deep Belly Breaths

Deep belly breaths are some of the best ways to relax yourself when you are struggling in the moment. Whether you are caught off guard or are completely unprepared for a situation ahead, breathing deep into your abdomen can help relax you. When we are in difficult or tense situations, we tend to get into a space where we are not breathing deep enough. We may even start breathing extremely shallow ones without even realizing it. If you need a quick activity to help you relax in the face of difficulty or uncertainty, deep belly breaths are a great opportunity. Simply breathe in deeply, hold it for a few seconds, and then exhale everything. This will help you release any tension or stress that you may be harboring inside.

Releasing Techniques

Releasing is one of the hardest but most important things we can do when we are experiencing difficult times. When you are going through a tough situation, it can be easy to absorb a variety of unwanted emotions and feelings without even recognizing it. You may even experience symptoms without having any realization as to what is happening. When you do, you need to release what is building up inside of you. Releasing can help you in many ways. It can help you alleviate difficult symptoms immediately, and it can also help you release unwanted emotions that remain after you have finished doing the difficult conscious work.

Visualization

When you are working on releasing unwanted feelings, energies and thoughts, visualization is one of the best practices you can use. You can use guided visualizations or guide yourself through your own visualization; it is completely up to you. To visualize something, you start by taking deep breaths and relaxing. Then, you can close your eyes and imagine yourself in your mind's eye. Picture what you look like and what the world around you will look like. The best part about visualization is that you can go anywhere you want and be anything you want. Visualize whatever makes you feel happy and positive inside. Then, you can visualize yourself releasing anything you're storing in a way that feels good for you. Some people choose to visualize their thoughts, feelings, or emotions as a cloud drifting away, whereas others choose to visualize it as a black smoke that is exhaled and eventually disappears. You may visualize yourself throwing it away or visualize it simply trickling away like a stream. You can make this visualization as personal to yourself as you desire. If you want to, you can follow a guided visualization, which may help you feel more focused if you are not experienced with visualization practices.

When you are visualizing, you will want to add as many senses as you can to the visualization. Imagine what the sights are, what sounds you might hear, and if there are any smells associated with the vision. If there is anything you feel, or taste, imagine that in your mind too. The more vivid you can make the experience, the better. This will make it truly feel as though you have honestly sent away anything you do not want to hold inside of you and will make the healing process much easier afterward.

Meditation

Meditation is always a powerful method for releasing unwanted thoughts, emotions, and feelings. Meditation is an excellent opportunity to quiet your mind when it is in a state of overwhelm or stress. You can meditate by taking deep breaths and closing your eyes. Stay focused on your breath and your body, and let all of your thoughts pass you by. Do not spend time judging the thoughts you have or obsessing over them; just let them come and then let them go again. When you do, they will pass by you easily. If you find yourself dwelling, obsessing, or judging, simply let go of the thought and judgment and then move on. The more you practice, the easier it will be. Let yourself stay in this state for as long as comfortable, and then gently guide yourself back into the room by opening your eyes and stretching out your body.

Deep Breathing

Deep breathing is an excellent tool for nearly any part of the mindfulness process. You can use it for releasing as well. When you are using deep breathing to release unwanted emotions, thoughts, or energies, imagine that each time you breathe out, you are exhaling everything that is unwanted. Then, every time you inhale, you are inhaling positivity, love, and peace. Spend some time taking these deep breaths and imagine the energies flowing in and out in this order until you are able to feel relaxed and released of any tensions or stresses you may be experiencing. You can use this tool as often as you need to achieve and maintain a peaceful state of mind.

Reframing

Sometimes, the best way to release something is to reframe the way you see it. Reframing is a process whereby you become mindful of the situation and work to see the positive in it. For example, imagine you experienced a red light on your way to work. You could curse and blame it for slowing you down. Alternatively, you could thank that red light for allowing you to take your time and experience the process of driving to work. You could appreciate that red lights, and traffic lights in general, are important tools that provide us with the ability to drive safely on the road without getting into accidents at every intersection. Reframing the way in which you see something is a great way to release tension, stress, frustration, anger, and any other unwanted emotion around it. You can reframe almost every situation simply by choosing to find positive elements of the situation and focusing on those instead of the negative elements.

Daily Practices

Mindfulness is best when you practice it on a regular basis. If you use mindfulness only when you feel triggered to or when you are experiencing heightened emotions, you will likely not get very far with your practice. You will also miss out on many of the amazing benefits and may struggle to develop your practice beyond a few thoughts. Daily mindfulness practices are a great way to increase your skills and see better results from your practices when you truly need mindfulness. You can use these mindfulness practices at least once a day, and they will help you increase the power of your practice immensely. Each practice does not take too long to complete, and you will find that you experience greater peace, freedom, and presence when you do.

Mindful Thinking

Thinking mindfully means that you not only become aware but also aim about the thoughts you have throughout the day. It may seem difficult, especially considering the amount of thoughts we experience on a daily basis. However, once you begin to practice this technique, you will likely find that it is a lot easier than you may think. The first step is to aim to think mindfully and to only have thoughts that serve your greatest good. Set the goal that anything that fails to serve your greatest good will be released effortlessly, and space will be cleared up for more positive thoughts. Once your goal is set, go about your day like you normally would. When you notice what thoughts you are experiencing, either feel happy that you are having positive ones or take action to release negative ones. Then, let yourself feel the joy of knowing that you have intentionally chosen your thoughts. Continue doing so throughout the day whenever you notice to do so. Eventually, you will find that, more often than not, you are completely aware of the thoughts you are having. You will also become aware of the times when your thoughts do not serve you, and you will be able to consciously change them into thoughts that will serve you. You may initially struggle to change your thoughts, and that's okay. The most important thing is that you feel confident and joyful every time you make a positive change. You do not want to punish yourself mentally or in any other way if you are not always successfully able to change your thoughts. Simply do your best and move on. Eventually, it will become extremely easy for you to change them. The most important thing is to practice on a regular basis.

Changing our thoughts can be one of the hardest things we do as humans. Many people feel as though their thoughts are things that are beyond their control and that they simply appear. The truth is, you have full control over your thoughts. You have the ability to shut down any thought you dislike and move on to a more positive thought if you so choose. Knowing that you have that power, you must understand that you also have the ability to increase the number of unwanted and negative thoughts you experience during the day. It is up to you to make the mindful and conscious choice of what thoughts you will support and which ones you won't. Then, take action and change your thoughts to better suit your ideal vision.

Mindful Awareness

Practicing mindful awareness means that you regularly take the time to honestly observe the situation you are in. You take the time to absorb what everything looks, sounds, feels, smells, and tastes like. When you get a gut feeling, you take the time to observe it. If something is particularly bright or patterned in an interesting way, you give yourself the time to observe it. Not only do you observe it, but you also observe the way you feel about it, whether it brings up positive or negative emotions or feelings for you. When you smell something, you take the time to discover whether it is a pleasant smell or a not so pleasant smell for you, and you take the time to explore the feelings it brings up. If you are listening to music, you take the time to listen to the sound and your reaction to the sound. You get the point: any time you are experiencing something and you become aware of the experience, take the time to truly, mindfully observe the experience. Let yourself become aware of what it feels like for you, what it looks like, and how it changes your emotions, if it does at all.

Mindful awareness is a great opportunity to explore your inner self deeper. It also gives you the ability to truly experience the world on a deeper level. When you practice mindful awareness, you stay in the moment and you experience more out of it. You become more skillful at your ability to truly stay in the moment, release stress, and lead a joyful and peaceful lifestyle. You don't have to practice mindful awareness 24/7, but practicing it on a regular basis is important. Whether you choose to practice it at a set time each day or when you feel prompted to by an external experience, the choice is yours.

Mindful Eating

Eating is a wonderful time to become mindful. These days, eating is less about the experience and more about the process of getting as much food down as you can that you don't feel full and then go rushing back to your busy life. This isn't true for everyone, but for many people, it is the case. Even if you don't find yourself rushing your meal, you can likely observe many instances where you do not actually take the time to fully experience your meal either. When you eat mindfully, you take the time to truly absorb the experience. You spend time looking at your food and smelling it, as well as truly tasting it. You chew slowly and swallow when you are done tasting everything in each bite. You take your time between bites and let yourself truly experience the entire moment. When you are full, you simply stop eating. You will likely feel a lot better after meals because you have eaten slowly enough that you can become aware of when you are full and you don't become ill a few moments later when you have eaten too much too quickly.

You can extend this mindful practice to drinking beverages as well. There is no need to gulp back water every now and again to ward off dehydration or when you feel like you can't go another moment without a sip. Instead, become mindful over your drinking habits. Watch as your cup fills with water, and spend time tasting the water as you drink it. Give yourself a chance to think about how the water feels in your mouth when you swallow it. Experience the entire process, and let yourself feel how great it is afterwards when you are done hydrating yourself. Both eating and drinking can be greatly enhanced by mindfulness practices. You prevent yourself from over eating or drinking too quickly and, as a result, increase the value you actually gain from your meals and beverages. You also reduce the chance of you feeling sick afterward.

Mindful Breathing

Breathing arises in every instance of mindfulness because it truly is a powerful practice. In daily mindful breathing, you do not need to become in control over your breath. There is no need to change the tempo, practice deep breathing, or count the breaths. Instead, you simply want to become aware of your own natural and unique breathing pattern. Spend time focusing on your inhalation and exhalation, and how your body feels when you take in and release the air as well. Let yourself fully experience what it is like to breathe and how your body feels when you absorb the oxygen. Imagine what it looks like when the oxygen purifies your cells and cleanses your system. Give yourself a few minutes to really think about your own unique breathing pattern.

If you do notice that your breathing seems shallow or that you are breathing in a way that does not feel comfortable for you, take the time to identify why you think your breathing is like that. Is it simply because you were not paying attention? Or do you feel any emotion that are causing you to have restricted or shallow breaths? If anything comes up, spend some time meditating on it and releasing it. Also, spend time focusing on your breathing pattern and bringing it back to a normal and fulfilling breath.

Mindful Appreciation

Gratitude is a powerful tool you can use to help increase the joy you experience in life. When you are mindful about appreciation and gratitude, you spend time purposefully acknowledging the things you have in life and showing appreciation for them. You acknowledge things no matter what size they are, and you spend time making sure that you show appreciation for them. You might show appreciation for your home, your car, the gas you fuel your car with, or even a pen that you use to fill out your daily journaling. You might want to show appreciation for family and friends, strangers who do kind things such as holding the door open, or stop lights that help guide traffic and keep everyone safe on the road. Mindful appreciation helps you realize the importance of everything in your environment and truly feel grateful for each item. When you show gratefulness and appreciation in this way, you become more joyful and attract more joy into your life. You aim to think positive thoughts that serve your greatest good, and you also aim to serve the greatest good of the collective.

Mindful Listening

Listening is sometimes an activity we take for granted. We listen to others only to formulate our own answers and opinions on what they are saying. We don't always hear exactly what they say because we are too busy hearing what we want to hear. This isn't always the case, but in many situations, it is. Very few people have strong, active, and mindful listening skills making them powerful listeners. When you listen mindfully, you listen with the aim to hear what you are being told. You do not formulate judgments or opinions until all of the information has been received, and even when in some instances, you do not formulate them at all. You spend time truly watching the person who is talking and understanding what they are saying to you. When you listen mindfully, you are aware of the emotions of the person who is speaking and the nonverbal communication they are sharing with you through their language. You hear the entire message, instead of snippets that stuck out to you.

When people take the time to mindfully listen, information is shared a lot easier. Relationships form deeper connections, arguments are avoided, and people feel heard and appreciated. Listening mindfully allows you the opportunity to truly understand the people you are communicating with and allows them the opportunity to truly feel understood. It is a great chance for you to absorb as much as possible from conversations you have and prevent possible miscommunications due to a lack of effective listening skills. This is a skill we often take for granted, but it is important that we learn to master it.

Body Scans

Daily body scans are a powerful way to tune into your body and feel into your emotions. These scans are mental examinations you do to your entire body: physical, emotional, and energy-wise. You take time to acknowledge how you are actually feeling. When we are busy in our daily lives, we tend to ignore our body and fail to listen to what it is telling us until it is quite literally screaming. We miss symptoms of illnesses until they become full-blown diseases, we miss symptoms of stress until we are no longer able to handle the pressure, and we miss many other things until we reach a point where we can no longer ignore them.

Think about a salt water tank. Each piece of life in the tank is vital to the survival of the entire tank. The fish, coral, and plants are all important, as well as the salt water and the sand. If any of the elements were missing or damaged, the entire tank would die. Hobbyists spend a small amount of time each day monitoring everything in the tank to ensure it is maintained properly. They adjust water temperatures and mineral levels, observe the living elements to make sure they are interacting well, and make any necessary changes to optimize the health of the entire tank. If the tank were left for even just a week, the levels could change drastically, and the entire tank would begin to spiral out of control. The water quality would dwindle, and the living elements of the tank would die off as well. Of course, if someone noticed the levels were off, they would likely be able to save it, but it would take drastic measures to do so. However, if they spent a little time each day maintaining the tank, they could avert any of these situations by recognizing them in advance and taking appropriate actions immediately.

Your body works in much the same way. Your physical body, emotions, feelings, energies, and everything else are all tied together. If one begins to suffer, the rest begin to suffer as well. Your body, emotions, feelings and energies will quickly spiral out of control until you reach a state where you either make a change or fade away to illness or otherwise. Of course, it takes us much longer than a week to completely spiral that far, and in many times, our bodies will give us major symptoms to indicate that we need to pay attention. However, the more we ignore, the worse the situation becomes.

A body scan works by taking a moment to relax and sit or lie down comfortably. Then, you start slowly considering how you feel in each part of your body, from the top of your head to the bottom of your feet. As you do, take note of any areas that may not feel good for you. Let yourself understand what these feelings are and where they come from. If you are feeling grief, for example, you may feel it in your chest area. If you are feeling dehydrated, you may feel it in your throat and head area. Any symptoms or feelings you are having will be felt somewhere in your body. When you do feel them, identify exactly where they are resting and spend time mindfully working through them and then releasing them. Give love to yourself and to any feelings you are having. Take the time to work through them. Manage your system before it is completely filled with toxicity and you are forced to tune in, in one way or another.

Many people believe that mindfulness is a highly spiritual practice, and for many people, it is. For others, however, it is a logical practice that is used to improve the quality of life and increase one's ability to cope with difficult situations. Regardless of how you choose to see the practices, they are highly beneficial and can add value to anyone's life. When you practice mindfulness on a regular basis, specifically on a daily basis, you increase the value you gain from your practice. You improve your life overall as your mental health and physical health increase. When you take the time to tune in and truly work through any issues you may be experiencing inside, you give yourself the opportunity to heal yourself and move on in life. You prevent yourself from becoming weighted down by difficult emotions or physical symptoms, and you move yourself into a space where you can heal and move on lightly. Mindfulness is a powerful practice to eliminate stress, promote peace and happiness, and teach people to live in the moment.

Chapter 5: Mindfulness Mastery

If you are someone who takes what you do seriously, you will likely want to know how you can go from "beginner" to "master". Of course, this book is a complete guide, and the goal is to teach you how you can become a mindfulness master. These techniques, tips, and guidelines are designed to help you understand how you can enhance your practice and increase the value you gain from it. These techniques are not necessarily all mindfulness practices on their own, but they are practices that will significantly enhance the quality of your own practice and, therefore, the results you gain from it.

Tips to Enhance Mindfulness Practice

When you are in the process of practicing mindfulness techniques, there are things that you can do to increase the value you gain from your practice. You can use these tips to make sure that your practice is successful and you get the most out of it that you possibly can. These tips are great for beginners who are looking to master the practice.

Slow Down

Some people want to practice mindfulness and master it all in the same day. While you can master mindfulness easily, the trick is not to rush yourself. The slower you go, the faster you'll master this practice. Using the techniques you have learnt in this book, take the time to teach yourself how to successfully do each one. When you find the ones that resonate with you, make these your "signature moves" and practice them frequently. Get to know them and how they serve you. Learn to understand what it feels like for you when you do this, and pay attention for opportunities to increase the quality of your results. Make it intimate and personal, and watch as your results explode. Slow down and take some of the pressure off of yourself. The process of mindfulness is largely related to the process of getting to know yourself, and as with any relationship, it takes time to truly become amazing at it. Give yourself the time to get there.

Focus on Concentration

A skill you should emphasize when you are learning about mindfulness and are wanting to master it is concentration. You should spend an enormous amount of time focusing on concentration when you are starting out, and you should seek to maintain your skill of concentration as you carry on. Concentration is a powerful tool that will help you stay focused on what you are trying to do and will prevent you from losing yourself to distractions. At first, distractions are rampant, and it is inevitable that you will become distracted in the process. To develop concentration, you can practice this skill all on its own. To do so, gather an object that you find intriguing to look at and place it in front of you. Look at the object and do your best to recognize all of the physical elements of the object. Observe the texture, color, shape, and size. Also observe your emotional and physical reactions to the object. Whenever you find yourself getting distracted, focus on the object again. Over time, you will find it much easier to focus on the object and stay focused for a long period of time. This focus and concentration will help you master everything using your mindfulness practice.

Start Simple

Relationships start with "hello" or something simple. The best relationships start with a small but sturdy foundation and gradually develop as one learn more about the other person, and everything grows from there. The same goes for mindfulness. Start with simple practices. Perhaps all you want to start with is recognizing when things trigger you and taking the time to become aware of your emotional and physical response to the trigger. Eventually, once you become practiced at recognizing the triggers, you will be able to implement a change to improve how you respond to the situation. When beginning, however, just stay focused on starting simple. The more you practice and successfully use mindfulness to change your life for the better, the easier it will be to use these techniques on larger and more emotionally charged situations.

Be Gentle on Yourself

Mindfulness should be a positive strategy that you use to eliminate stress and stay present in the moment. Being harsh on yourself when you do not succeed to your desired standards will do the exact opposite; it will get you stuck in your head and cause you to stress out. Instead, be gentle and kind to yourself. If you recognize a trigger several moments, hours, or even days after it occurred, don't become angry with yourself for not recognizing it in the moment. Instead, celebrate yourself for recognizing it at all. The same goes for any goal you have with mindfulness. Maintain the positive associations with the practice by being gentle to yourself and celebrating all of your wins. Use "losses" as a milestone: events that occurred, which taught you a lesson about yourself and your life. Then, absorb the information from the lesson, so you can use it in the future. We all take time to get from point A to point B, and you are no different. Be kind to yourself and your practice will flourish in no time.

Be Patient with Yourself

For the same reason why you want to be gentle to yourself, you should be patient too. If it takes you several weeks to successfully complete goals you have set out for yourself, don't get stressed because it is taking you longer than you desired. It is likely that you are learning a great deal about yourself along the way and that you are gaining more than you could have possibly imagined when you embarked on the journey. Give yourself time, and let yourself embrace each experience. A large part of being mindful is being able to recognize that you are not always in control of the situation, and sometimes, you will benefit from letting go completely and simply going with the flow of things. Again, the slower you go, the faster your practice will develop. Be easy on yourself, and refrain from setting any timelines with your goals. As long as you are making steady progress, consider that a success and keep doing what you are doing. If you notice areas where you may be able to improve your practice to increase your success, of course, do so. But do not feel that a slower pace is the result of failure. It is absolutely not true. Be patient with yourself.

Learn to Let Go

Many people struggle to let go of things, and a big part of being mindful is learning to let go. There are many instances where you will be triggered, but there will be absolutely nothing you can do. The mindful approach to these situations is to learn to let go. Use the releasing techniques taught in this book, and release the emotions or feelings you have generated around the experience. You are not required to hold on to everything that you experience in life. Whether you had emotional or mental work to do around the situation or not, when all is said and done, learn to effectively let go. At first, you might struggle with this as we tend to hold on to the things that affect us. This is because on a biological level, the things that hurt us are a "threat", and we must avoid them to be able to survive. The reality is that we are far more advanced than that, and the majority of our perceived threats really are not threats at all. A good idea is to have a set period of time each day where you let go of the day. Anything that has upset you, stressed you out, or otherwise taken up space in your mind can be released, and you can allow yourself to thoroughly relax and rest for the night. When you do this, you will find that you sleep better, and your stress levels are much lower overall.

Make It Fun

You wouldn't stay friends with someone who was too serious or boring, would you? Mindfulness does not have to be a serious or boring experience. In fact, there are many ways that you can incorporate mindfulness into your life and make it a thrilling experience. One of the best practices for mindfulness is learning to stay in the present moment. When you stay present in the moment, you experience the moment much greater. Use your practice in moments that present a great amount of joy and happiness, and you will absorb an unbelievable amount of that. There is no reason for the practice to be all boring and serious all of the time. While you are going to want to stay present in difficult moments and work through those as well, it doesn't have to be all about that.

Adjust It to Suit Your Needs

Everyone is different in many ways. There are no two people who are exactly the same. As a result, you should recognize that your mindfulness practice will not be the same as others either. You will find that some techniques work better than others for you, and over time, you will develop your own unique concoction of techniques and strategies that will fulfill your needs. Take your time and feel free to adjust as necessary. Believe it or not, you will likely be adjusting your strategies and tactics for your entire life when you are practicing mindfulness. As we grow and evolve, our needs do as well. As a result, so does our mindfulness practice.

Tips for Staying Committed

Some people struggle to stay committed to new habits. The reality is that mindfulness is a complete lifestyle change. You cannot achieve mindfulness and then have it forever; instead, you must work to keep the balance of mindfulness in your life on a regular basis. The following tips are great for helping people stay committed to their practice.

Practice for at Least 21 Days

They say it takes 21 days for something to officially become a new habit. That being said, if you take the time to practice mindfulness for at least 21 days, it will become a new habit in your life. If you can commit yourself to three weeks of practicing mindfulness on a daily basis, you will find that by the end of the three weeks it comes as a second nature to you. Then, it will be much easier to remember to do it on a regular basis.

Set a Reminder in Your Phone

For some people, an easy way to remember is to set a reminder in your phone. Choose the time of day that best suits your needs, and set the reminder. Then, when your reminder goes off, take a few minutes to practice mindfulness. If you are someone who tends to be busy or if you want to learn to practice mindfulness in your active life and not just when you have the time to have a break, you might want to consider setting several reminders. Have one for the morning, afternoon, and night. Then, whenever the reminder goes off on your phone, you will remember to be mindful over the present situation. This is a great way to ensure that you remember to practice mindfulness.

Have Anchors or Triggers

Some people are not so fond of phone reminders or may not feel that it is enough to help them practice it frequently. If this is the case, you can consciously aim that certain situations, objects, or other anchors will trigger you to practice mindfulness. For example, maybe you aim that every time you see an analog clock you will become mindful over the situation. At first, you may forget about this, but later on, you will find that every time you see an analog clock, you start practicing a mindfulness technique and become more present in the moment. You can set as many or as few anchors as you would like, and they can be anywhere and made from anything. You might choose a piece of jewelry, a certain object you see on a regular basis, or even a specific person to be your anchor. It is completely up to you.

Journal Your Progress

Another great tool for encouraging you to stay committed is a journal. Journals are excellent for helping you track and record your progress throughout the experience. For some people, being able to write down their experiences throughout the day is a great opportunity to remember to practice mindfulness. Whenever you see the journal, you will remember to become mindful, and then, you will be able to track your experience. Then, you have a trigger as well as written proof of just how far you have come.

There are many ways that you can improve your mindfulness practice to help you grow from being a beginner to being a master. The key is to take it slow, get to know your own unique practice, and do whatever you need to in order to stay consistent and committed to the practice. Once you do it long enough, you will start to learn more about yourself and your own unique practice, and soon enough, it will become easier for you to master.

Conclusion

Mindfulness is a powerful practice that can completely transform your life. When you use the tools of mindfulness, you give yourself the opportunity to reduce the amount of stress you experience and teach yourself to become more present in the moment. As a result, you will find that you are more peaceful, positive, joyful, and optimistic in life. You may not be able to completely relieve yourself of all stressors, but you will be able to totally change the way you respond to stressors, which will have a huge impact on your health and well-being.

I hope *Mindfulness for Beginners: Secrets to Getting Rid of Stress and Staying in the Moment* was successful at helping you learn how you can eliminate your stress and stay present in the moment. This book was designed to empower people to feel more confident in not only starting up their own mindfulness practice but also mastering it. Remember, the slower you go and the more you practice and stay committed, the sooner you will become a master and the greater results you will see from your practice.

The next step is to start from the beginning. Take your time and start developing your mindfulness practice by developing your concentration skills and learning to become self-aware of moments as they happen. As you feel more and more comfortable with your practice, you will be able to advance to greater steps and start making real and noticeable changes in your life. Then, your life will transform in front of your very eyes, and you will see how easy it is to control yourself and your reality.

Lastly, if you enjoyed this book, I hope that you will take the time to honestly rate it on Amazon Kindle. Your honest feedback would be greatly appreciated.

Thank you, and good luck.

Help me improve this book

While I have never met you, if you made it through this book I know that you are the kind of person that is wanting to get better and is willing to take on tough feedback to get to that point. You and I are cut from the same cloth in that respect. I am always looking to get better and I wish to not just improve myself, but also this book. If you have positive feedback, please take the time to leave a review. It will help other find this book and it can help change a life in the same way that it changed yours. If you have constructive feedback, please also leave a review. It will help me better understand what you, the reader, need to make significant improvements in your life. I will take your feedback and use it to improve this book so that it can become more powerful and beneficial to all those who encounter it.

Free membership into the Mastermind Self Development Group!

For a limited time, you can join the Mastermind Self Development Group for free! You will receive videos and articles from top authorities in self development as well as a special group only offers on new books and training programs. There will also be a monthly member only draw that gives you a chance to win any book from your Kindle wish list!

If you sign up through this link http://www.mastermindselfdevelopment.com/specialreport you will also get a special free report on the Wheel of Life. This report will give you a visual look at your current life and then take you through a series of exercises that will help you plan what your perfect life looks like. The workbook does not end there; we then take you through a process to help you plan how to achieve that perfect life. The process is very powerful and has the potential to change your life forever. Join the group now and start to change your life!
http://www.mastermindselfdevelopment.com/specialreport

You will also love these other great titles from Mastermind Self Development!

You will want to check out these other great titles Mastermind Self Development. All available in the Kindle store or you can just click on covers below.

getBook.at/mindfulnessforbeginners

http://mybook.to/positive

You can also find these titles by searching them in the Kindle store on Amazon.